Contents

Schofield & Sims English Skills 2

GU00870173

SECTION 1

Spelling: Vowel phonemes; less common digraphs (**ph, ch**); less familiar letter so_____ ____ **wash**). High-frequency words. Common letter patterns (**le** endings); rules for adding **ing** and **ed** (double consonants); basic plural spellings. Syllables.

Word structure: Compound words. Prefixes (**un, dis**); suffixes (**ful, ly**).

Vocabulary: Synonyms for high-frequency words; using syntax and context to work out meaning; cross-curricular words.

Sentence structure: Forming simple sentences, questions, exclamations, compound sentences. Extending sentences (using connectives).

Punctuation: Demarcating sentence boundaries; full stops, capital letters, question marks, exclamation marks. Commas that separate items in a list.

Grammar: Past tense; agreement. Identifying nouns; improving noun choice. Identifying verbs; selecting verbs for sentences.

SECTION 2

Spelling: More plural spelling rules; more rules for adding **ing, ed**. Silent letters; spelling rules for adding suffixes.

Word structure: Prefixes (**mis, re, pre**) and suffixes (**less, able**). Forming adjectives (adding **y**). Forming comparatives (adding **er, est**).

Vocabulary: Choosing more interesting words; synonyms; antonyms. Inferring meaning from word structure and context; technical and subject-specific words.

Sentence structure: Developing ideas within a sentence. Writing separate linked sentences; introducing more connectives.

Punctuation: More uses of capital letters. Using commas to separate lists of adjectives or phrases. Speech marks.

Grammar: Imperatives. Plural forms. Identifying and selecting adjectives, and understanding their purpose.

SECTION 3

Spelling: Plural spelling rules (**f, ves**). Rules for verb endings. Medium-frequency words. Shortened forms with apostrophes.

Word structure: More prefixes, focusing on meaning. More suffixes, focusing on usage; rules for adding vowel suffixes.

Vocabulary: Homonyms. Improving word choices. Writing definitions; using context and word structure to work out meaning.

Sentence structure: Combining ideas in one sentence. Conjunctions; using connectives at the start of sentences. Using connectives to link sentences.

Punctuation: Punctuating dialogue. Using sentence punctuation effectively. Using commas to mark grammatical boundaries.

Grammar: First and third person. Plural forms. Pronouns. Improving choice of adjectives, nouns and powerful verbs; relating choice to purpose.

A WARM-UP

1 Write a sentence using these words only.

moon the landed The rocket on

_____

Put the letters in order to make two words.

2 t h e a   _ _ _ _   and   _ _ _ _

3 a e m n   _ _ _ _   and   _ _ _ _

Write a question using these words.

4 **bears honey**

_____

5 **trees winter**

_____

Add the missing letters.   _Clue: days of the week_

6 M _ n d _ y

7 S _ t _ r d _ y

8 W _ d n _ s d _ y

9 Th _ rsd _ y

10 T _ _ s d _ y

B WORD WORK

Write two compound words starting with **some**.

1 some _____

2 some _____

Write three words that mean the same as the word in **bold**.

3 **little** house   _____ _____ _____

4 I was **happy**.   _____ _____ _____

Underline the word that is wrongly spelt.
Write the correct spelling.

5 The King frownd.   _____

6 The crowd gaspt.   _____

7 Clouds floatid by.   _____

Add the missing syllable.

8 l e m ___ a d e

9 d i ___ s a u r

10 h e l i ___ t e r

C SENTENCE WORK

1 Write this message without using the word **and**.

We went to the city farm and we saw a baby lamb and he was lovely.

_____

2 Circle the four capital letters.   On Saturday I saw Molly in town.

Write down why the capital letter was used.

3 _____

4 _____

5 _____

6 _____

Use the words to make a question.

7 Jack did win. _____

8 I can do that. _____

9 They will come. _____

10 You must go. _____

X There is only one correct answer.   X **There is more than one correct answer.**

Section 1   Test 2 ✓

A   WARM-UP

1   Write a sentence using these words.

dog duck

_____

Use these words to make four compound words.

spoon   pot   cake   pan   tea   dust

2 _____   **4** _____

3 _____   **5** _____

Write the pairs of words that rhyme.
Add another word to each pair.

snail great day whale grey late

6 _____ , _____ and _____

7 _____ , _____ and _____

8 _____ , _____ and _____

9   Put these words in order to make a sentence.

you I that help with can

_____

10   Make a question using the same words.

_____

B   WORD WORK

Add the correct plural ending.

1   short ____

2   jean ____

3   sunglass ____

Write the meaning of the word in **bold**.

4   The monster's face was **hideous**.

'hideous' means _____

5   The water **glistened** in the sun.

'glistened' means _____

6   The car had been **abandoned**.

'abandoned' means _____

Write four words that start with **ph**.

7   ph _____

8   ph _____

9   ph _____

10   ph _____

C   SENTENCE WORK

What punctuation mark is hidden by the symbol?

I have my pencil■ ruler■ crayons and book▲

1   ▲ _____

2   ■ _____

3   Add four items to complete the sentence.

I went shopping and I bought _____

Change the words in **bold** to make a new sentence. Write the new sentence.

4   A **cloud** floated in the **sky**.   _____

5   **James** dropped the **jelly**.   _____

6   A **cat** crept through the **grass**.   _____

Write the sentence correctly.

7   he goed home   _____   **9**   we was in a hurry   _____

8   she must of lost it   _____   **10**   were are you   _____

Section 1 Test 3

A WARM-UP

1 Write a sentence using these words only.

shook the girl her head little

_____

The same vowel sound is missing from all these words. Write it in.

2 s t ___ m   **4** c ___ n

3 l ___ d   **5** t ___ c h

Write two more words with the same spelling of the vowel sound.

6 _____

7 _____

Write the pairs of words with the same spelling pattern. Add another rhyming word.

brother would another could

8 _____ , _____ and _____

9 _____ , _____ and _____

10 Write a question with these words in it.

elephant trunk

_____

B WORD WORK

Underline the correct spelling.

1 peeple   peopel   people   peepul

2 tippt   tipped   tiped   tipt

3 dishis   dishes   dishs   dishies

Write two words that mean the same as the word in **bold**.

4 **cold**   _____ _____

5 **fast**   _____ _____

6 **old**   _____ _____

7 **sad**   _____ _____

Write three words that start with **ch** when it sounds as it does in the name **Chris**.

8 _____

9 _____

10 _____

C SENTENCE WORK

Read this aloud.   **the rain poured down everyone was soaked the picnic was ruined**

1 How many sentences did you hear?   _____

2 Write the sentences with full stops and capital letters.

_____

Add **but** or **so**.

3 He found the door _____ it was locked.   **5** It is cold _____ it is not raining.

4 He found the door _____ he could escape.   **6** It is cold _____ wrap up warm.

Write the sentence in the past tense.

7 This week, we go on holiday. Last week, _____ .

8 Today it rains. Yesterday _____ .

9 The dragon snarls. Then _____ .

10 Complete the sentence and add any punctuation marks that are missing.

Inside the chest there was a magic mirror thirty coins a string of beads

and _____

6   X There is only one correct answer.   X There is more than one correct answer.

Section 1   Test 4

A   WARM-UP

Write six sentences using these words only.
Use three words in each sentence.

he we they was were happy cold

1 _____

2 _____

3 _____

4 _____

5 _____

6 _____

Make two four-letter words using these letters only.

7 **r d a e**   _____ and _____

8 **a e r t**   _____ and _____

Use these words to make two compound words.

fly green house

9 _____

10 _____

B   WORD WORK

Add the missing syllable.   *Clue: colours*

1 s c a r ____   3 e m ____ a l d

2 b u r ____ d y   4 v i _ l e t

5 The same letter is missing from all these words.
Write it in.

w _ s h   w _ n t   w _ s

Write the meaning of the word in **bold**.

6 a woodland **habitat**
a 'habitat' is _____

7 Flowers **produce** seeds.
'produce' means _____

8 Fruit **contains** seeds.
'contains' means _____

Underline the word that is wrongly spelt.
Write the correct spelling.

9 It was abowt five o'clock.   _____

10 The howse seemed empty.   _____

C   SENTENCE WORK

Add the missing punctuation and capital letters.

1 I watched the match last night did you see it

2 ben ella samir megan and sarika were in my group

3 did you hear about ryan he broke his arm

Cross out the word that is wrong. Write it correctly.

4 I woked up early today.   _____

5 The wind blowed.   _____

6 We all weared our PE kit.   _____

Add to these sentences to say **where** each event happened.

7 We saw the car _____

8 A plane landed _____

9 The man hid _____

10 Write the notes as one complete sentence.

tadpole – young frog   _____

X There is only one correct answer.   X There is more than one correct answer.

7

Section 1   Test 5

A WARM-UP

Write a sentence using these words.

1 dog roof

_____

_____

2 Gran sunglasses

_____

_____

3 animal motorway

_____

_____

Add the missing letters.   **ir er ur or**

4 b ___ d   **6** w ___ k

5 c h ___ c h   **7** h ___ b

Make three questions.

8 _____ is your name __

9 _____ do you live __

10 _____ old are you __

B WORD WORK

Make six words using these words and prefixes only.

able like please un dis well

Write the word beside its meaning.

1 _____   ill or sick

2 _____   annoy or upset

3 _____   put out of action

4 _____   hate

5 _____   not able to do something

6 _____   different

Underline the correct spelling.

7 brushis   brushes   brushs

8 wishis   wishs   wishes

These words have the same spelling pattern.

giggle puddle wobble drizzle

9 What is the pattern?

_____

_____

10 Write two more words with this pattern.

_____   _____

C SENTENCE WORK

1 Add three items.   In my sandwich I had _____

Write an ending for the sentence.

2 We left early but _____

3 We left early so _____

Underline the verb.

4 Lizards eat insects.

5 Tigers hunt at night.

6 Hummingbirds hover near flowers.

7 Chimps swing through trees.

Add capital letters and full stops.

8 the wind turned icy lucy shivered she hated the cold

9 it was getting late mr brown frowned and looked at his watch

10 mark lay in bed he listened for a moment it all seemed quiet

8   X There is only one correct answer.   X There is more than one correct answer.

Section 1　Test 6

A　WARM-UP

Put the words into rhyming pairs.
Add another word to each pair.

stair fear door peer more bear

1 _____ , _____ and _____

2 _____ , _____ and _____

3 _____ , _____ and _____

4 Change the words in **bold** to make a new sentence.

   Butter is made from **cream**.

   _____ is made from _____ .

Make six sentences using some of these words only.

I she we is are am brave late

5 _____

6 _____

7 _____

8 _____

9 _____

10 _____

B　WORD WORK

Write these verbs so they end with **ing**.

1 drum_____   4 whirl_____

2 hook_____   5 bob_____

3 spit_____   6 hear_____

Write these sentences with all the words spelt correctly.

7 We wotcht the swons and swollows.

   _____

8 She pickt up the boxis foor him.

   _____

Sort the verbs into two groups.

amble   dart   dash   plod

trudge   sprint   saunter   tear

9 **run** _____

10 **walk** _____

C　SENTENCE WORK

Write a sentence using these words.

1 **bark and cat** _____

2 **home but road** _____

3 **gold but cave** _____

Add a verb.

4 The man _____ in a puff of smoke.

5 They all _____ happily ever after.

6 The door _____ open.

Write the sentence correctly.

7 **the giant strided over the hill**

8 **someone must of lost it**

9 Is this a sentence? **The little grey rabbit.**

10 Give a reason for your answer.

_____

_____

_____

_____

X There is only one correct answer.　　X There is more than one correct answer.

9

Section 1 Test 7

A WARM-UP

1 All the words have the same letters missing. Write them in.

ar er or ir ur

w___t h   w___s e

w___k   w___l d

Write a question using these words only.

2 **is it dark night why at**

_____

3 **fizzy lemonade is why**

_____

Add **un** or **dis** to make a new word.

4 ____t r u s t   6 ____s e l f i s h

5 ____h a p p y   7 ____a g r e e

Add the missing letters.

Clue: found in the garden

8 b _ t t _ _ _ f l y

9 d _ n d _ l _ _ n

10 c _ t _ r p _ l l _ r

B WORD WORK

1 Underline the three words that mean the same as **looked**.

glanced glared nudged peered jerked

Add another word to make a compound word.

2 farm_____

3 snow_____

4 play_____

Make the noun into a plural.

5 one dish   → three _____

6 one plate   → three _____

7 one lunchbox   → three _____

8 one glass   → three _____

Add the same suffix to all three words.

9 hope____   pain____   wish____

10 smooth____   kind____   sudden____

C SENTENCE WORK

Cross out the verb and write one of these instead.

collapsed swaggered heaved

1 He put the sack onto his back.   _____

2 The bridge fell.   _____

3 The pirate went down the road.   _____

Add a question mark or an exclamation mark to the end of the book title.

4 Look out__

5 Oh no, Joe__

6 Why does the wind blow__

7 Can I__

8 Whose shoes__

9 Stop thief__

10 Complete this sentence.

Plants have roots so _____

X There is only one correct answer.   X There is more than one correct answer.

A WARM-UP

1 Change the words in **bold** to make a new sentence.

All **elephants** have **trunks**.

_____

Add the missing letters. *Clue: months*

2 N _ v _ m b _ r   **4** J _ n _ _ r y

3 S _ p t _ m b _ r   **5** F _ b r _ _ r y

Make four new words out of these words and suffixes.

ly ful fear power

6 _____   **8** _____

7 _____   **9** _____

10 Write two sentences. Use one of these words in each.

cake mess

_____

_____

B WORD WORK

Write the meaning of the word in **bold**.

1 Suddenly someone **yanked** my arm.

'yanked' means _____

2 The King was well **protected**.

'protected' means _____

Cross out the words that are wrongly spelt. Write the correct spellings.

3 Her dad werks all over the werld.

_____ _____

4 Use the handel to lift the kettel.

_____ _____

5 He startid to wosh the dishis.

_____ _____ _____

Write the verb with the **ed** ending added.

6 **train** _____

7 **trot** _____

8 **snap** _____

9 **tap** _____

10 **leap** _____

C SENTENCE WORK

Write a noun in each space to complete the sentence.

1 Three _____ were sitting on the old _____ by the _____ in the farmyard.

2 From the beach we could see _____ bobbing in the _____ near the _____.

3 In the supermarket, a _____ with a _____ was standing by the _____.

Write the sentence as a short exclamation.

4 I need some help. _____

5 I think he will go bananas. _____

6 Suddenly there was a crash. _____

Add the capital letters.

7 on saturday i went to see manchester city play aston villa.

8 on sunday i went to simeon's house in west burton.

Complete the sentence.

9 Ice-cream starts to melt when _____

10 Water freezes when _____

Section 1   Test 9

A   WARM-UP

Use the letters to make two words.

1 a e c r   _____ and _____

2 e o r s   _____ and _____

3 Write a sentence using these words.

cupboard but empty

_____

_____

4 Add four nouns to complete the sentence.

In the garden we saw beetles, _____

_____

Make four compound words ending with **room**.

5 _____   **7** _____

6 _____   **8** _____

Add the missing letters.

9 O n _ e   u p _ n   a   _ _ _ _ _

10 H a p _ i l _   e v _ r   a f t _ _

B   WORD WORK

1 What spelling rule do these words follow?

snagged spinning spotted dragging

_____

_____

_____

Give two more examples.

2 _____   **3** _____

Write three nouns that name types of

4 shop _____ , _____ , _____

5 road vehicle _____ , _____ , _____

6 dog _____ , _____ , _____

7 sportswear _____ , _____ , _____

Add the correct prefix. Then write the meaning of the new word.

un dis non

8 ____ trust   means _____

9 ____ sense   means _____

10 ____ popular   means _____

C   SENTENCE WORK

Cross out the word **came** and use one of these words instead.

swarmed slithered trickled

1 Water came out of the pipe.   _____

2 The ants came out of the hole.   _____

3 The snake came across the floor.   _____

Add the correct punctuation mark at the end of the line.

4 **Mum:** Shall we have beans for tea__

5 **Child:** NO__

6 **Mum:** But you like beans on toast__

7 **Child:** NO__

8 **Mum:** Well, what about spaghetti then__

Finish the sentence.

9 Goldilocks ran away because _____

10 Little Bear was angry because _____

X There is only one correct answer.   X There is more than one correct answer.

Section 1 Test 10

A WARM-UP

Put the words into rhyming pairs.
Add another rhyming word.

burn moon born prune learn lawn

1 _____ , _____ and _____
2 _____ , _____ and _____
3 _____ , _____ and _____

Write a sentence, a question and an exclamation
using the word **spaceship**.

4 **sentence** _____

_____

5 **question** _____

6 **exclamation** _____

Add the missing vowels.

Clue: numbers

7 s _ v _ n t _ _ n   9 _ l _ v _ n
8 f _ _ r t _ _ n   10 _ _ g h t _ _ n

B WORD WORK

Add to each sentence a verb ending with **ing**.

1 Ducks were _____ about
on the water.

2 Ed was _____ the branch
behind him.

3 The man is _____ his head
in agreement.

4 I felt you _____ my shoulder.

Add the missing letters.

5 g r _ _ n h _ _ s e
6 p l _ y g r _ _ n d
7 l i _ _ t h _ _ s e

Write two words to use instead of **said** which could
show that a person was

8 **speaking loudly** _____ _____
9 **speaking quietly** _____ _____
10 **speaking happily** _____ _____

C SENTENCE WORK

Use one of these nouns in place of the crossed-out word.

office cottage theatre palace

1 The King waited in his ~~house~~.   _____
2 The fisherman waited in his ~~house~~.   _____
3 The businessman hurried into the ~~building~~.   _____
4 The actor hurried into the ~~building~~.   _____

Finish the sentence.

5 The post office was closed when _____
6 The post office was closed so _____
7 The post office was closed because _____

Add the capital letters and punctuation.

8 it began to snow soft flakes gently landed on sarah's hair

9 suddenly there was a loud sound boom what was it

10 what is your favourite sort of dog is it a poodle a greyhound a collie or a bulldog

X There is only one correct answer.   X There is more than one correct answer.   13

Section 1 Test 11

A WARM-UP

Finish the sentence.

1 Dogs bark when _____

2 I feel happy when _____

Read the words aloud. Underline the odd one out.

3 hear   beard   bear   near

4 Give a reason for your choice.

_____

_____

Add the missing syllable. *Clue: sports*

5 a t h _____ i c s

6 b a d _____ t o n

7 g y m _____ t i c s

8 s w i m _____

Write a sentence and a question using these words only.

swim can bears polar

9 sentence _____

10 question _____

B WORD WORK

1 What spelling rule do these words follow?

dishes passes fizzes matches

_____

_____

Write two more words that follow the same rule.

2 _____   **3** _____

4 The same letter is missing from all these words. Write it in.

s w _ l l o w   s w _ p   w _ n d e r

Write two verbs that mean the same as

5 jump   _____ _____

6 shine   _____ _____

Add a prefix and a suffix.

un dis ful ly

7 ___ fair ___

8 ___ like ___

9 ___ help ___

10 ___ trust ___

C SENTENCE WORK

Add a word to complete the sentence.

hunted hurled hurtled huddled

1 Adam _____ his toys away.

2 Our dog Ziggy _____ into the lake.

3 Lucy _____ by the fire to keep warm.

4 Deepak _____ for his rucksack.

Underline the nouns.

5 The boys packed tents, sleeping bags and a powerful torch.

6 What do these words tell us about what the boys are going to do? _____

7 Change the nouns to make a new sentence.

The _____ packed _____

Write the sentence/s correctly.

8 Nina tom and sacha lives in george street _____

9 I red two book last week what about you _____

10 He were late he must of misst the bus _____

☒ There is only one correct answer.   ☒ There is more than one correct answer.

A WARM-UP

Add a word to complete the sentence.

1 The car _____ suddenly.

2 Everyone _____ happily.

3 The same phoneme is missing from all these words. Write it in.

f___m e r   h___m f u l   g___d e n

Add a prefix and a suffix.

4 ___fair___   ___grate___

5 Look at how these words end. Underline the odd one out.

double   label   table   bubble

6 Give a reason for your choice.

_____

Write four compound words that start with **sun**.

7 _____   9 _____

8 _____   10 _____

B WORD WORK

Write the meaning of the word in **bold**.

1 It was not what he **intended**.

'intended' means _____

2 She was **irritated** by my remark.

'irritated' means _____

3 He **trudged** back up the hill.

'trudged' means _____

Add **un** or **dis** to make new verbs.

4 ___ own   6 ___tie

5 ___fold   7 ___ infect

8 What spelling rule do these words follow?

baking striding sparkling

_____

Write two more examples of words following this rule.

9 _____   10 _____

C SENTENCE WORK

1 Underline the nouns in the sentence below.

2 Then draw a ring round the verbs.

The seagulls squawked loudly as the waves crept across the sand.

3 What setting does the sentence describe? _____

Change the nouns and verbs so that the sentence describes

4 **a wood**   The _____ loudly as the _____ across the _____.

5 **a street** The _____ loudly as the _____ across the _____.

Finish the sentence by adding words that say **when** the event happened.

6 Kerry woke up _____

7 They ran outside to play _____

8 We piled into the car _____

Write the notes as a complete sentence.

9 **all birds – wings**   **not all fly**   _____

10 **Monday – sunny**   **Tuesday – rain**   _____

Now complete Section 1 of the Progress chart on page 46.

X There is only one correct answer.   X There is more than one correct answer.   15

Section 1 Writing task: Sam gets lost

Task

You are writing a story about Sam. He went out for the day with his family, but then he got lost. Write a paragraph describing the moment he realised he was lost. Describe what Sam saw and how he felt.

Hints

Before you start:

- Choose a setting.
- Think about the event.
- Imagine what Sam saw and heard.

- Consider how Sam felt.
- Make notes on some of the words you might use.

As you write, think about:

- The words you choose.

- The sentences you write.

Sam looked around.

Check

- When you have finished, check through your story.
- Have you checked the punctuation and spelling?
- Does everything sound right?

Section 1 Proofreading task: My camping diary

Task

Read through this diary entry.

Change anything that does not look or sound correct.

Hints

- Do the sentences sound right?
- Is the punctuation correct?
- Do all the spellings look right?

we arrivd at camp on sataday. I was shareing a tent with ben adam and Harvey.

Mick was unnable to come. becuwse he were not well.

Furst we had to lern how to put up our tent. we wotcht mr jenkins demastrate

and then we had a go adam took a foto off us when the tent was finaly up.

It was just then that it startid to rayn we all huddeled in our tent the

rayn kept comeing it were geting werse and werse it was druming on the canvas

and there was a huge puddel of warter forming on the roof of the tent suddenley

somethink snapt and the tent collapset on top of us we was all sowkt

Extra

Now write a diary entry for the next day.

Section 2 Test 1

A WARM-UP

Write two sentences for a story. Use one of these nouns in each sentence.

farmer tree

1 _____

2 _____

3 Underline the odd one out. *Clue: spelling*

  hissing   stepping   nodding   thudding

4 Give a reason for your choice.

  _____

  _____

5 Cross out the nouns. Write new nouns.

  Smoke drifted in the air. _____ _____

Write three compound words ending with **thing**.

6 _____thing

7 _____thing

8 _____thing

Add the missing phoneme to make two rhyming words. **are eer**

9 g l_____ and s t_____

10 c h_____ and j_____

B WORD WORK

These words and prefixes are mixed up.
Write them correctly.

unbehave **mis**obey **im**lucky **dis**possible

1 _____   3 _____

2 _____   4 _____

5 How do the prefixes change the meanings of the words?

  _____

6 What spelling rule do these words follow?

  spies teddies parties

  _____

  _____

  _____

7 Write another word that follows the same rule.

  _____

Write the meaning of the word in **bold**.

8 **settlement** _____

9 **population** _____

10 **occupation** _____

C SENTENCE WORK

Add the connecting word.

while   until   after   since

1 Jack was glad to be home _____ his adventure.

2 Someone had broken in _____ they were out.

3 They walked _____ they could go no further.

4 Jason had been an unusual child _____ birth.

Underline the verb and change it to the present tense.

5 Leo lived on a far away island. _____

6 Something tapped on the window. _____

7 Emma and Lucy were friends. _____

Add the capital letters.

8 florence nightingale was born in florence in italy.

9 turn left into park street at simmond's supermarket.

10 i enjoyed 'snip snap', which is the new book by sam jackson.

X There is only one correct answer.   X There is more than one correct answer.

A WARM-UP

1 Change the first part of the sentence.

~~The wind howled~~ but I was safe in the hut.

_____

2 Write a sentence using these words.

milk but cat

_____

_____

3 The same phoneme is missing from all these words. Write it in.

bef ____   m ____   sh ____line

Add the missing syllable to complete the list of rhyming words.

4 tum ____   grum ____   rum ____

5 mud ____   pud ____   cud ____

6 bub ____   trou ____   stub ____

Add a word to make a compound word.

7 luke _____   **9** draw _____

8 wheel _____   **10** horse _____

B WORD WORK

Underline the correct plural spelling.

1 donkeys   donkies   donkyes

2 puppys   puppies   puppyes

3 witchis   witchies   witches

Underline the suffix that you can add to all the words. Write it in.

4 ly est ful

quick ____   long ____   kind ____

5 ful less ly

care ____   end ____   friend ____

6 ly less er

rich ____   kind ____   tall ____

Synonyms are words with similar meanings. Write two synonyms for the word in **bold**.

7 a **silly** idea   _____ _____

8 a **fierce** beast   _____ _____

9 the **moody** boy   _____ _____

10 a **bright** light   _____ _____

C SENTENCE WORK

Cross out the nouns. Write new nouns to make the sentence more interesting.

1 A man rode a bike along the road.   _____ _____ _____

2 The dog jumped from the wall into the bush.   _____ _____ _____

3 The woman took the dog to the shop.   _____ _____ _____

4 The boy crossed the road to reach the shop.   _____ _____ _____

Add more to each instruction so it says exactly **where**.

5 Sieve the flour _____

6 Bake the pie _____

7 Sprinkle sugar _____

What punctuation mark is hidden by the symbol?

▲We need biscuits■ eggs■ cereal and milk■ ▼ said Mum◆

8 ▲ ▼ = _____

9 ■ = _____

10 ◆ = _____

X There is only one correct answer.   X There is more than one correct answer.   19

Section 2 Test 3

The beginnings and endings of these sentences are mixed up.

All books	**is fiction.**
Some books	**have pages.**
A storybook	**has a glossary.**
This book	**are non-fiction.**

Write the sentences correctly.

1 _____

2 _____

3 _____

4 _____

Make four compound words. *Clue: clothing*

suit sweat over pull track coat shirt

5 _____   7 _____

6 _____   8 _____

Use the letters to make a different word.

9 **t h i n g**   _ _ _ _ _

10 **n o w**   _ _ _

Write the phrase so that the verb ends with **ing** and the noun is plural.

1 make jelly   _____

2 drop catch   _____

3 smile face   _____

4 Add a prefix to make an opposite.

____tidy   ____honest

____visible   ____bug

Use the words in these sentences.

5 This room is _____ .

6 He had a _____ face.

7 The wizard made himself _____ .

8 We had to _____ the computer.

Write the meaning of the word in **bold**.

9 It was an **enchanting** evening.

'enchanting' means _____

10 He had to **obey** the King's wishes.

'obey' means _____

Add capital letters and full stops.

1 a fish is an animal with a tail and fins it lives in water

2 gently heat the mixture add the fruit stir until it is hot

3 the lights went out there was a thud someone screamed

Finish the sentence.

4 When you toast bread _____

5 When you run very fast _____

6 When you press the brakes on a bike _____

Cross out the verb. Write a new and more interesting verb.

7 He went through the brambles.   _____

8 The monster looked at him.   _____

9 The thunder banged.   _____

10 Everyone ran away.   _____

X There is only one correct answer. X There is more than one correct answer.

Section 2   Test 4

A   WARM-UP

1 Write the sentence using different nouns.

The burglar stole a painting from the

museum. _____

_____

Change one phoneme to make the word match
the meaning.

2 peer _____ means **not rich**

3 flat _____ means **to drift**

4 drown _____ means **to scowl**

5 have _____ means **to pull**

Underline the word that is a synonym of the
word in **bold**.

6 **kind** mean cruel caring unkind

7 **strong** weak mighty frail feeble

8 **boring** exciting dull thrilling

9 **ill** untidy sick messy well

10 The same syllable is missing from all these
words. Write it in.

v a n ___ p u n ___ a s t o n ___

B   WORD WORK

1 Add the same prefix to all three words.

un re de dis

___play ___fill ___write

2 How does it change the meaning?

_____

3 Write two more words with this prefix.

_____ _____

Write two verbs that mean the same
as the verb in **bold**.

4 **laugh** _____ _____

5 **eat** _____ _____

6 **pull** _____ _____

7 **weep** _____ _____

Cross out the words that are wrongly spelt.
Write the correct spelling.

8 Two lorrys were driveing arownd.

_____ _____ _____

9 Some childrun were droping litter.

_____ _____

10 It is allways coola at nite.

_____ _____ _____

C   SENTENCE WORK

Add **after**, **when** or **until**.

1 We watched TV _____ it was bedtime.

2 We watched TV _____ tea.

3 We watched TV _____ we came in.

4 Underline the verbs in these instructions.

Add the banana. Beat with a wooden spoon. Empty the yoghurt into a bowl. Stir well.

5 How are verbs used in instructions? _____

Write four reasons why capital letters have been used in this sentence.

Mr Jackson's class was silent. Then suddenly ... CRASH!

6 _____

7 _____

8 _____

9 _____

10 Write this sentence in the past tense. **He knows it is late.** _____

X There is only one correct answer. X There is more than one correct answer. **21**

Section 2   Test 5

A   WARM-UP

Change the underlined words.

1 After they paddled in the sea,
   <u>Nathan and Sophie</u> made a sandcastle.

   _____

2 _____

   <u>When Sultan heard the roar,</u> he began
   to run.

These words and suffixes are mixed up.
Write them correctly.

properful **speech**ly **bead**less **wish**y

3 _____   **5** _____

4 _____   **6** _____

Add the missing vowel phoneme.

ea ee ie oa

Clue: used in place of **said**

7 s c r ___ m e d   **9** g r ___ n e d

8 s c r ___ c h e d   **10** s h r ___ k e d

B   WORD WORK

1 What do the words have in common?
   know write half lamb

   _____

2 What is the letter that is hidden?
   ■new   ■now   ■neel   ■nit   _____

3 Add an **ed** ending.
   chuckle _____   **cry** _____
   giggle _____   **sob** _____

Write the new words as pairs of synonyms.

4 _____ and _____

5 _____ and _____

Write the meaning of the word in **bold**.

6 **disqualify** _____

7 **revisit** _____

8 **predict** _____

Sort the movement verbs.

**creep thrash crawl scramble
scuttle charge drift edge**

9 **slow** _____

10 **fast** _____

C   SENTENCE WORK

Add a word to join the sentences. Do not use **and**.

1 Jack climbed _____ he reached the top.

2 It was dark _____ he took a torch.

3 The kite took off _____ the wind blew.

Underline the adjectives.

4 There was once a beautiful princess who lived in a sparkling palace on top of a high,
   misty mountain.

5 A thistle is a wild plant with purple flowers and prickly leaves.

6 What is the purpose of adjectives?

   _____

Add anything that is missing.

7 "can I come?" said the little girl

8   I can help you, said the mouse.

9 "What are you doing?" _____

10 "You shall go to the ball," _____

X There is only one correct answer.   X There is more than one correct answer.

Section 2 Test 6

A WARM-UP

1 Extend the sentence so that it says **where** the Prince ran.

The Prince ran _____

2 Add more so that it says **where and why**.

The Prince ran _____

_____

Write four compound words ending with **ball**. Write them in alphabetical order.

3 _____   **5** _____

4 _____   **6** _____

Underline the word that is **not** a synonym.

7 **shine**   gleam   fade   glint

8 **brave**   bold   daring   weak

9 **quick**   fast   fine   swift

10 The same two-letter word fits into all these longer words. Write it in.

w _ _ r e   t _ _ r e   _ _ l p

B WORD WORK

1 Complete the word sum.

1 **baby** × 2 = _____

1 **child** × 2 = _____

1 **mouse** × 2 = _____

1 **fox** × 2 = _____

2 Add **er** and **est**.

small   _____ _____

rich   _____ _____

pale   _____ _____

Use one of the words you have made.

3 The Moon is _____ than the Sun.

4 He was the _____ man in the land.

5 Pink is a _____ colour than red.

6 The King was _____ than the beggar.

Add the missing vowels.

Clue: found in food

7 f _ b r _   **9** v _ t _ _ m _ n s

8 c _ r b _ h y d r _ t e s   **10** s _ g _ r

C SENTENCE WORK

Cross out the verb. Choose and write a new one.

produces powers pumps

1 The heart sends blood round the body.   _____

2 Electricity works many machines.   _____

3 The honeybee makes the honey we eat.   _____

Write three adjectives that describe the item in **bold**.

4 Try this fresh, _____ _____ _____ **bread**.

5 Try this _____ _____ _____ **ice-cream**.

6 Try this _____ _____ _____ **sports car**.

Write the notes as one complete sentence.

7 **dragonfly – insect – lives near water** _____

8 **windows – glass – light pass** _____

9 **windmill sails – turn – power** _____

10 **spider – web – food** _____

A WARM-UP

The beginnings and endings of these sentences are mixed up.

Some dogs	**moves round the Sun.**
Frogs	**dig holes.**
An artist	**eat flies.**
The Earth	**paints pictures.**

Write the sentences correctly.

1 _____

2 _____

3 _____

4 _____

Underline the odd one out.

5 untrue uniform unfair unlock unreal

6 disagree distrust disallow dishes disorder

7 repay reform recycle reread really

8 Give a reason for your choices.

_____

Add a word to complete the longer word.

9 u n _____ f u l

10 d i s _____ i n g

B WORD WORK

Add the missing syllable.

Clue: buildings

1 h o s _____ a l

2 s u p _____ m a r _____

3 f a c _____ y

4 Add the suffix **y** to make the word an adjective.

crunch _____

luck _____

sun _____

stone _____

Use one of these adjectives to complete the phrase.

5 _____ day   7 _____ number

6 _____ ground   8 _____ apple

Write the meaning of the word in **bold**.

9 The people were **alarmed** by the blaze.

'alarmed' means _____

10 The gates **prevent** him from entering.

'prevent' means _____

C SENTENCE WORK

Underline the adjectives.

1 The surface of the moon is dry and dusty.

2 Mercury is a small, hot, rocky planet.

3 Saturn is a large planet with bright rings.

4 Why have these adjectives been used in this piece of factual writing?

_____

Add the correct punctuation.

5 What shall we do asked the little girl.

6 Who's been sitting in my chair said father bear.

7 Help shouted Jack.

Finish the sentence by adding information that explains.

8 Don't stand behind a moving swing _____

9 Eat lots of fruit and vegetables _____

10 We keep milk in a fridge _____

X There is only one correct answer. X There is more than one correct answer.

A   WARM-UP

1   Write a sentence using these words.

paint but ladder

_____

_____

Add the missing letters.

er ir ur

Clue: kinds of movement

2   w h ___ l   4   c ___ l

3   s q u ___ m   5   j ___ k

6   Finish the sentence by giving a reason.

The old man smiled _____

_____

Add three letters to complete the word.

7   _ _ _ c k l e

8   _ _ _ c l e

9   _ _ _ d l e

10   _ _ _ b l e

B   WORD WORK

Make an adjective from the word in **bold** and use it to complete the sentence.

1   A bear has **fur**. It is _____ .

2   The silver coin **shines**. It is _____ .

3   The film was **fun**. It was _____ .

4   **Snow** is falling. It is _____ .

5   All these words have the same spelling pattern.

know knew knife knock

What is the pattern?

_____

Write three more words with the same pattern.

6   _____   8   _____

7   _____

Write two antonyms (opposites) for the word in **bold**.

9   The Prince was **kind**.

_____   _____

10   The shop was **neat**.

_____   _____

C   SENTENCE WORK

Cross out the nouns and write them as plurals. Write the new sentence so that it makes sense.

1   Waiting inside was a woman with a baby and a schoolchild.

Waiting inside _____

2   The old lady had a bad foot. _____

Finish the sentence.

3   The party went well until _____

4   As he made his wish, _____

Add the full stops and capital letters.

5   a plant is a living thing it has a stem, leaves and roots most plants grow in the earth

6   march is the third month it has 31 days it is named after the roman god mars

7   it was late dylan had not come home bj and bella were waiting for him

Cross out the verb. Write a new verb that fits the mood.

8   The angry dog barked at the stranger.   _____

9   The grumpy old man talked to himself.   _____

10   He happily went down the road.   _____

X There is only one correct answer.   X There is more than one correct answer.   25

Section 2 Test 9

A WARM-UP

1 Underline the word that is **not** an adjective.

smooth   rough   rock   hard   powdery

2 Why is it not an adjective?

_____

3 Add a suffix to make it an adjective.

_____ + _ = _____

Change the verb to make a new sentence.

He smiled at the boy.

4 _____

5 _____

Write four compound words that start with **under**.

6 under_____   **8** under_____

7 under_____   **9** under_____

10 The same two-letter word fits into all these longer words. Write it in.

u p___   s e c__d   ___e

B WORD WORK

Add **er** and **est**.

1 crazy   _____   _____

2 flat   _____   _____

3 kind   _____   _____

4 gentle   _____   _____

Write the meaning of the word in **bold**.

5 This paper is **absorbent**.

'absorbent' means _____

6 The glass is **transparent**.

'transparent' means _____

7 The plastic is **opaque**.

'opaque' means _____

Cross out the words that are wrongly spelt. Write the correct spellings.

8 Sudenly I stopt.

_____   _____

9 It has a grate nuty taste.

_____   _____

10 Take harf a pear and two hole cherrys.

_____   _____   _____

C SENTENCE WORK

Use one of these words to replace the words in **bold**.   cavity   molars   bacteria

1 Your **big back teeth** are used to chew food.   _____

2 Brush your teeth or **germs** will grow.   _____

3 You may get a **hole** in your tooth.   _____

4 Underline the adjectives.

The alien had an enormous head with round, bulging eyes. Its tiny body was covered in red pointed scales. It had a short brownish tail with a green tuft on the end.

Write each adjective beside the type of thing it describes.

5 colour   _____   _____   _____

6 size   _____   _____   _____

7 shape   _____   _____   _____

Complete the sentence so that it says **when** the event happened.

8 _____ Abdul had a slice of apple pie.

9 _____ the farmer became rich.

10 The snow melted _____

X There is only one correct answer.   X There is more than one correct answer.

Section 2 Test 10

A WARM-UP

1 Add the suffix **y** to make an adjective.

powder _____

gloss _____

dust _____

shine _____

Write the words as pairs of synonyms.

2 _____ and _____

3 _____ and _____

Add the missing vowels.   *Clue: time connectives*

4 b _ f _ r _

5 m _ _ n w h _ l _

6 s _ n c _

7 _ n t _ l

8 Write a sentence using these words.

mouse when cat

_____

_____

Write the notes as two complete sentences.

chess – board game – 64 squares

9 _____

10 _____

B WORD WORK

1 Underline the silent letter.

k n e e   g n a t

c r u m b   w r i n k l e d

Add the missing syllable.

2 d i f ____ e n t

4 t o ____ r o w

3 i n ____ i g e n t

5 a n i ____

6 Add the same suffix to all the words.

ful ly able less

enjoy_____   drink_____   read_____

Use two of the words in this sentence.

7 The book was _____ and _____

Write three synonyms for the word in **bold**.

8 **pretty** _____ _____ _____

9 **sly** _____ _____ _____

10 **scary** _____ _____ _____

C SENTENCE WORK

Add the punctuation and capital letters.

1 who wants an ice-cream asked melanie

2 me screamed bobbie and robbie

3 what flavour do you want there is mint or vanilla explained melanie

Rewrite the sentence so it sounds like an instruction.

4 We had to beat the eggs with a fork.   _____

5 The milk and sugar were added to the eggs.   _____

6 We baked it for 25 minutes.   _____

Continue the sentence in four different ways.

7 Martha had very little money so _____

8 Martha had very little money because _____

9 Martha had very little money until _____

10 Martha had very little money but _____

X There is only one correct answer.   X There is more than one correct answer.

A   WARM-UP

Continue the sentence.

1   The ball bounced _____

_____

2   The boy slipped _____

_____

Make three words using these
letters only.

e i d t

3   _ _ _ _   *Clue: changes in the sea*

4   _ _ _ _   *Clue: the food you eat*

5   _ _ _ _   *Clue: made a knot*

Add a short word to complete the longer word.

6   t o ___ h e r   8   s u d ___ l y

7   b ___ o o n   9   f o l ___ i n g

10   Add the same phoneme to all the words.

   or ea ear air

   s ____ c h   ____ t h   l ____ n

B   WORD WORK

Complete the word sums.

1   greed + y = _____ + est = _____

2   sun + y = _____ + est = _____

3   skin + y = _____ + est = _____

4   scare + y = _____ + est = _____

Write three nouns that name types of

5   **aircraft**   _____ _____ _____

6   **storm**   _____ _____ _____

7   **bird**   _____ _____ _____

Write the pairs of words
with the same spelling pattern.
Add another similar word.

found would sound should

8   _____ , _____ and _____

9   _____ , _____ and _____

10   Cross out the words that are wrongly spelt.
Write the correct spellings.

   Carefuly slice the strawberrys.

   _____ _____

C   SENTENCE WORK

Add the missing words to the dialogue. It begins, **"When will we see the sea?" asked Jamie.**

1   _____ replied Dad.

2   _____ shouted Jamie excitedly.

Write the notes as one complete sentence.

3   **mole – small animal – soft fur – underground**

_____

4   **frog – smooth, moist   toad – dry, rough**

_____

5   **wheat → flour → bread** _____

Cross out the verbs in the present tense. Write them in the past tense.

6   I visit my dad and he takes me out.   _____ _____

7   The farmer runs and hides behind a rock.   _____ _____

8   The wizard sits and writes in his book of spells.   _____ _____

9   The Prince stops and grabs his sword.   _____ _____

10   The girl sees the old lady but says nothing.   _____ _____

[X] There is only one correct answer.   [X] There is more than one correct answer.

A   WARM-UP

Cross out the nouns. Write new nouns to make a new sentence.

1 A bull has horns.

_____ _____

2 Tom was an elf who lived in a wood.

_____ _____ _____

Underline the correct spelling.

3 runy   runny   runnie

4 happiest   happyest   happyist

5 riseing   rissing   rising

Add different prefixes to the word **cover** to make three new words.

6 ____cover

7 ____cover

8 ____cover

9 Look at the separate parts of these words. Underline the odd one out.

without   inside   something   follow   anyone

10 Give a reason for your choice.

_____

B   WORD WORK

1 Add the silent letter.

_ n i f e   _ r i t e

h a _ f   a n s _ e r

2 Add the suffix **able**.

enjoy_____   value_____

agree_____   comfort_____

Use the words in these phrases.

3 a _____ armchair

4 an _____ day out

5 a _____ diamond ring

6 a pleasant and _____ man

7 Add the vowels.   *Clue: weather*

r _ _ n f a l l   d r _ _ g h t   t _ r n _ d _

Use the words in these sentences.

8 A _____ tore up the trees.

9 There has been little _____.

10 There may soon be a _____.

C   SENTENCE WORK

1 Write two sentences for a story. Use one of these words in each sentence.   **frog river**

_____

2 Write two sentences for a report. Use one of the same two words in each sentence.

_____

Write the notes as two complete sentences.   **leopard – cat family   lives – Asia   forests – climbs trees**

3 _____

4 _____

Add adjectives.

5 The house was _____ and _____ with a _____ door and _____ garden.

6 The _____ man had a _____ face with _____ eyes.

7 The sky was _____ with _____ clouds covering the _____ moon.

Add the capital letters and punctuation.

8 our senses allow us to see feel taste hear and smell things.

9 i must warn the king said ivan.

10 don't do it shouted maria

Now complete Section 2 of the Progress chart on page 46.

X There is only one correct answer.   X There is more than one correct answer.

Section 2 Writing task: Dressed for the weather

Task

Write two paragraphs for a report called **Dressed for the weather**. The full report will give information about what clothes to wear in different countries at different times of year. Your writing should focus **either** on two different countries **or** on two different times of year in the same country.

Hints

Before you start, think about:

- The information you want to give.
- How you will organise your report.

As you write, think about:

- The words you choose.
- The sentences you write.

Check

- When you have finished, check through your report.
- Is the punctuation correct?
- Have you checked your spelling?

Section 2 Proofreading task: The lost treasure

Task

Read through this story.

Change anything that does not look or sound correct.

Hints

- Do the sentences sound right?
- Is the punctuation correct?
- Do all the spellings look right?

The stoney path twistid up into the mowntains there was a fearfull rumbul far away

but clara new she had to folow the path there was no terning back. She was glad

she had her map sord and majic clowk with her.

Clara scrambuld up the steap path untill she was lost in the mists and clowds suddunley

the path became flata and the mist cleered clara fownd she was standin by the bigist

cave she had ever seen. She creeps up to the edje of the cave. And peers inside.

Just at that moment there was a mightey roor and a powerfull voyce. Who dares come

to the cave of zog? it cryed.

Extra

Now write an ending for the story. Think carefully about the words and sentences you use.

Section 3 Test 1

A WARM-UP

Add the missing syllable. *Clue: shapes*

1 p y ___ m i d   3 r e c ___ g l e
2 h e x ___ g o n   4 t r i ___ g l e

Finish the sentence.

5 The monster ate _____

_____

6 He lived in a cave _____

_____

7 He roared _____

_____

8 The monster was sad _____

_____

Sort the words into two sets of synonyms.

sturdy weak powerful feeble

powerless frail burly strong

9 _____

10 _____

B WORD WORK

1 What spelling pattern do these words share?

write wreck wrinkle wrong

_____

Write four more words with same pattern.

2 _____   4 _____
3 _____   5 _____

Add a suffix to each word. Write it in one of the sentences.

mouth amaze

6 He tasted a _____ .
7 He looked round in _____ .

Write three synonyms of the word in **bold**.

8 The man wore **nice** clothes.

_____ _____ _____

9 The burglar **went** up the path.

_____ _____ _____

10 There was a **sound** of machinery.

_____ _____ _____

C SENTENCE WORK

Cross out a verb or verb phrase and use one of these instead. **hibernate migrate survive**

1 Many animals find it hard to live in winter.   _____

2 Some of them go to sleep.   _____

3 Some birds fly away.   _____

4 Why are the new verbs better choices?   _____

Write the sentence as a line of dialogue.

5 Ben asked his mum for help.   _____

6 Josh shouted hello to Ravi.   _____

7 Katie asked the time.   _____

8 Add the capital letters and full stops.

emily turned there was a wolf he was standing right behind her

9 Rewrite the sentences as one complete sentence.

_____

10 Write another sentence that says what happened next.

_____

X There is only one correct answer.   X There is more than one correct answer.

Section 3   Test 2

1 Add the missing silent letters.

cas__le   s__ord   r__yme

Make four words using these words and suffixes only.

cheer quiet ful ness er y

| 2 _____ | 4 _____ |
| 3 _____ | 5 _____ |

The beginnings and endings of these sentences are mixed up.

Fish work in schools.
Teachers bark loudly.
Some dogs have humps.
Camels live in water.

Write the sentences correctly.

6 _____

7 _____

8 _____

9 _____

10 Make two words using these letters only.

a s w   _____ and _____

1 What is missing from these words?

dont isnt Ive weve

_____

_____

Write the shortened forms correctly.

| 2 _____ | 4 _____ |
| 3 _____ | 5 _____ |

Write a synonym of the word in **bold**.

6 He was a **troublesome** boy.   _____

7 That's **precisely** what I meant.   _____

8 He was **dumbfounded**.   _____

Sort the words into two groups.

caring thoughtful heartless spiteful
unfeeling ruthless considerate unselfish

9 kind   _____

_____

10 cruel   _____

_____

Complete the sentence. Add commas where they are needed.

1 Mrs Gill shut the front door locked it put the key in her bag and _____

2 Tom stamped his feet flung down his bag screwed up his face and _____

3 The magician stood up waved his wand said the magic words and _____

Use one of these words to complete the sentence.   **if since though**

4 I like playing football _____ I'm not that good at it.

5 We have lived here _____ I was five.

6 I know I will do it _____ I keep trying.

Read this.   **The man went out of the building. The wind blew.**

How could you make the sentences more interesting? Explain two ways.

7 _____   8 _____

Improve the sentence.

9 The man went out.   _____

10 The wind blew.   _____

X There is only one correct answer.   X There is more than one correct answer.   **33**

A WARM-UP

1 Write a sentence using these nouns.

giant flower garden

_____

_____

Add the missing letters.

Clue: parts of your hand

2 w r _ _ _   4 k n _ _ _ _ _ _

3 t h _ _ _

5 What do the words have in common?

_____

Add the missing letters.

er ear ir ur

6 t h ____ s t y   8 m i s h ____ d

7 h ____ t f u l   9 a f t ____

Add more information about the event.

10 Ruby remembered _____

_____

B WORD WORK

Add these suffixes to the word **happy**.

ness er est ly

1 _____   3 _____

2 _____   4 _____

Add verb endings.

5 We went swim_____, sunbathe_____
   and paddle_____.

6 They came run_____, skid_____ and
   hurtle_____ into the playground.

7 Write a synonym of the word in **bold**.

   gruffly   _____

   immensely   _____

   gleefully   _____

Use the synonyms in these sentences.

8 The little boy laughed _____.

9 The task was _____ difficult.

10 "Why?" he asked _____.

C SENTENCE WORK

Add the punctuation and capital letters.

1 mr marshall found a dusty old picture in his house in lexton somerset

2 was it worth anything the answer is yes

3 mr marshall told our reporter, I was most surprised to hear it was valuable

Underline the verbs.

4 The man's eyes flashed as he glared at Simon.   5 He stomped around, muttering to himself.

6 What do these verbs tell us about the character? _____

Write the sentences with different verbs to change the mood of the character.

7 _____

8 _____

Rewrite the information in one sentence.

9 Stir the mixture. Use a wooden spoon. Stop when it is golden brown.

_____

10 A bat is a small animal. It looks like a mouse. It has wings.

_____

34   X There is only one correct answer.   X There is more than one correct answer.

Section 3   Test 4

A   WARM-UP

These words and suffixes are mixed up.
Write them correctly.

goodless hair**ful** regret**ness**

1 _____   **3** _____

2 _____

Finish the sentence.

4 While she waited, _____

5 As darkness fell, _____

Add the missing letters.

oar our ar

6 p____ e d   **8** s w ____ m e d

7 s ____ e d

Change the verbs.

9 They strolled down the road,
     laughing and joking.

_____ _____ _____

10 Trees whispered and waved in the wind.

_____ _____

B   WORD WORK

Write the words in their shortened form.

1 **does not**   _____

2 **she has**   _____

3 **I would**   _____

4 **will not**   _____

5 Underline the prefix.

   disconnect   misplace   rearrange

Write a definition (the meaning).

6 'disconnect' means _____

7 'misplace' means _____

8 'rearrange' means _____

Sort the words into two groups.

**red purple lavender mauve scarlet
burgundy cherry violet lilac crimson**

9 _____

10 _____

C   SENTENCE WORK

Underline the pronouns.

1 My sister was waiting so I picked up my bag and we left.

2 We will meet you at the end of your road with our bikes.

3 She was so late that they grew restless waiting for her.

4 He invented it in his workshop.

Cross out any unnecessary adjectives.

5 They warmed their icy hands by the boiling hot fire.

6 He lived in a great big, huge, enormous mansion.

7 Why are the extra adjectives not needed?

_____

Continue the sentence about a story you have read.

8 I have chosen this story because _____

9 You will enjoy this story if _____

10 I liked the story though _____

Section 3 Test 5

A WARM-UP

Add a short word to complete the longer word.

1. in____mation
3. char____er
2. inte____ing
4. con____ue

5. Use these words to make five compound words.

   in out ways with side

   _____

Add a word to the sentence.

6. The hare was _____ than the tortoise.

7. A book is _____ than a feather.

8. A mango is _____ than an apple.

9. What do all the words have in common?

   _____

10. Write a sentence using these verbs.

    snarled wriggled

    _____

    _____

B WORD WORK

Add a suffix to the word in **bold** so that it matches the definition.

1. **cheer**_____   sad and gloomy

2. **harm**_____   dangerous

3. **child**_____   silly

4. **near**_____   almost

Change the nouns into plurals.

5. The leaf fluttered on the branch.

   _____   _____

6. We took the loaf off the shelf.

   _____   _____

7. The furry bunny rode in the buggy.

   _____   _____

Use one of these words in the sentence.

structure inflatable reclaimed

8. This airbed is _____.

9. We built a tall _____.

10. We used _____ materials.

C SENTENCE WORK

Add punctuation to the dialogue.

1. Have you remembered the box asked Julia.

2. We are nearly there said Max.

3. That's it shouted Nick Let's go

4. Be careful Its very icy warned Joe.

Use one of these connectives to replace **then**.

After that, Suddenly, Eventually

5. It was a long journey. Then _____ they arrived.

6. We watched the match. Then _____ we had tea.

7. They fell asleep. Then _____ the phone rang.

Improve the report by changing the words in **bold**. Write the sentence with the new words in place.

8. We **got** the rainwater in the **pot**.   _____

9. Then we can **see how much rain there is**.   _____

10. We **put** the **numbers** on a **paper**.   _____

36   X There is only one correct answer.   X There is more than one correct answer.

Section 3　Test 6

A　WARM-UP

Write four words ending with **ness**.

| 1 _____ | 3 _____ |
| 2 _____ | 4 _____ |

5　Add the correct double letters.

h o ___ l e

g i ___ l e

g u ___ l e

Continue the sentence.

6　King Crumble was happy if _____

_____

7　King Crumble was happy because _____

_____

8　King Crumble was happy until _____

_____

9　King Crumble was happy so _____

_____

10　King Crumble was happy though _____

_____

B　WORD WORK

Write the correct spelling.

1　**crum** _____

2　**rino** _____

3　**rubarb** _____

4　Why were the spellings wrong?

_____

Write the sentence correctly.

5　Its the hotist day ov the yeer!

_____

6　Ive seen a famly of foxis

_____

7　He droppt the rapper in the rode.

_____

Write an adjective that is stronger than the word in **bold**.

8　It was a **horrible** sight. _____

9　The book was **interesting**. _____

10　She was **surprised**. _____

C　SENTENCE WORK

Add a comma.

1　Food helps us to grow gives us energy and keeps us healthy.

Add three phrases to complete the sentence.

2　An elephant uses its trunk to _____

3　Seeds are dispersed by _____

_____

Add pronouns.

4　Charles Dickens was a writer. _____ wrote many novels. _____ were very popular.

5　Ducks are birds that swim. _____ have webbed feet. Many of _____ feed in fresh water.

6　Milk comes from cows. _____ is an important food. _____ gives _____ protein and minerals.

Choose two connectives to use in instructions and two to use in a story.

Next, At that moment, Continue to, But meanwhile

7　**instructions** _____　8　**story** _____

Continue the sentence.

9　The shadowy figure disappeared. Minutes later _____

10　Sieve the flour into the bowl. Next _____

X There is only one correct answer.　X There is more than one correct answer.

Section 3   Test 7

A WARM-UP

Write an antonym.

1 inflate _____

2 input _____

3 equal _____

Write each noun as a plural.

4 puppy   kitten   mouse

_____   _____   _____

5 prince   princess   wolf

_____   _____   _____

Add more information about the event.

6 He waited outside the bank _____

_____

7 He opened the chest carefully _____

_____

Add the missing vowel phoneme.

Clue: *they sound like a sound*

8 c r ___ k   10 w h ___ s h

9 b l ___ p

B WORD WORK

1 Complete the verb sum.

scurry + **ed** = _____

display + **ed** = _____

replay + **ed** = _____

reply + **ed** = _____

2 What spelling rule did you use?

_____

_____

Write the verb beside the correct definition.

construct examine recommend magnify

3 _____   look at closely

4 _____   enlarge

5 _____   build

6 _____   suggest

Add the same prefix to all three words.

7 ____ freeze   ____ septic   ____ clockwise

8 ____ read   ____ behave   ____ understand

9 ____ -stick   ____ -fiction   ____ sense

10 ____ claim   ____ plain   ____ change

C SENTENCE WORK

Add the missing punctuation and capital letters.

1 dear mrs jenkins

you are a winner you have won first prize in our competition

2 hi joss

we will meet you and andy at penley station on saturday see you then

3 dear mr clarke

i enjoyed greatly your book cold times you are my favourite author

Choose the one adjective that works best and cross out the others.

4 The cute kiwi is a brown flightless bird.   5 The scary stripy tiger is a powerful creature.

How did you choose the adjectives to cross out? Give two reasons.

6 _____

7 _____

Cross out the words that do not sound right. Write the correct words.

8 "I is hungry," said the alien. "What does you eat on you planet?" _____ _____ _____

9 "I likes it here. Everyone are very friendy to my." _____ _____ _____ _____

10 "I thinks there is lots more peoples for I to meet." _____ _____ _____ _____

38   X There is only one correct answer.   X There is more than one correct answer.

Section 3   Test 8

A   WARM-UP

Write a sentence using these words.

1   **moon dog street** _____

_____

2   **water park kite** _____

_____

Write three words that rhyme with the word in **bold**.

3   **chair** _____ _____ _____
4   **four** _____ _____ _____
5   **turn** _____ _____ _____

Sort the connectives into two groups.

Just then, Finally, Later,

At once, Eventually, Suddenly

6   **In the end** _____
7   **Right then** _____

Complete the word chain.

cold colder coldest

8   hot _____ _____
9   fast _____ _____
10 heavy _____ _____

B   WORD WORK

Write a definition of the word in **bold**.

1   We went on a **train**.

   train: _____

2   We **train** daily for the race.

   train: _____

3   She put the **ring** on her finger.

   ring: _____

4   A bell began to **ring**.

   ring: _____

5   What do you notice about the words **train** and **ring**?

_____

Write the word with the apostrophe in the correct place. Then write the full form.

6   **shell'** _____ _____
7   **well'** _____ _____
8   **were'** _____ _____
9   **shed'** _____ _____
10 **youd** _____ _____

C   SENTENCE WORK

Write these lines so that the **said** part is in the middle of the dialogue, not at the end.

1   "What are you doing here? This is private land," said the man.

_____

2   "I am Zoll. I come from the planet Kroll," said the alien.

_____

3   "Sophie, I want to speak to you," said Mum.

_____

Write a word to use instead of **said**. Make the character sound angry.

4   _____ the man   6   _____ Mum
5   _____ the alien

Read the sentence. Pretend you are Oscar. Write the sentence in the first person.

7   Oscar sold his mother's best cooking pot.   _____
8   It belonged to Oscar's mother not to him.   _____
9   Should Oscar give the money to his mother?   _____
10 Or should he keep it for himself?   _____

Section 3   Test 9

A   WARM-UP

Change the nouns so the sentence gives a different picture.

1   A man stood by the door holding a briefcase.

_____ _____ _____

2   The fox followed the chicken into the farmyard.

_____ _____ _____

3   The baker put the cake in the oven.

_____ _____ _____

Add **ee** and/or **ea** to complete the word.

4   s___w___d   6   s w___t h___r t

5   c h___r l___d e r   7   h___d g___r

Underline the two words in each list that have more than one meaning.

8   ice   spot   day   chin   bat

9   light   ear   wave   flour   big

10   rose   frog   leaves   grass   bud

B   WORD WORK

Write a more formal synonym for the word in **bold**.

1   **Stick** it to the wall.   _____

2   It was a **nice** view.   _____

3   Underline the prefix.

demist   debug   defrost

4   What does the prefix mean?

_____

Make the word into a plural.

5   **lady** _____   7   **hobby** _____

6   **diary** _____   8   **baby** _____

9   What rule did you use to help you?

_____

_____

10   Add the missing syllables.

Clue: finding and bringing together

d i s_____e r i n g   c o l_____i n g

C   SENTENCE WORK

Improve the sentence by changing the words in **bold**.

1   We hope to **do up** the school library.   _____

2   Mrs Hawkins will **give** the prize.   _____

3   We hope to **make** some money.   _____

4   Why are your words better than the words in **bold**? _____

5   Add two full stops and two exclamation marks.

SLAM Everyone stood very still Yes, it was a magic carpet No-one moved for a long time

6   Why did you decide to use exclamation marks where you did?

_____

7   Write the sentence again so that it starts with the word **while**.

The snow began to fall while everyone slept. _____

Finish the sentence.

8   As the snow fell on the houses, _____

9   When the people awoke, _____

10   Because it was so cold, _____

☒ There is only one correct answer.   ☒ There is more than one correct answer.

A WARM-UP

Finish the second sentence.

1 Jack searched for the gold. Before long,

_____

2 Jack searched for the gold. Meanwhile,

_____

Write two synonyms for the word in **bold**.

3 **shake**   _____ _____

4 **hungry**   _____ _____

5 **creep**   _____ _____

Add the missing phoneme.

Clue: light

6 g l ___ m   8 g l ___

7 s p ___ k l e   9 b ___ m

10 Write a sentence using these words.

   cat bowl suitcase

_____

B WORD WORK

Write a definition of the word in **bold**.

1 They began to **row** down the river.

_____

2 We put out a **row** of chairs.

_____

3 There was a terrible **row** afterwards.

_____

What do you notice about the word **row**?

4 _____

5 _____

These words and suffixes are mixed up.
Write them correctly.

bagable relyful painy

6 _____   8 _____

7 _____

Correct the spelling.

9 Peepul shud laff moore.

_____

10 The teem playd betta in the furst harf.

_____

C SENTENCE WORK

Continue the sentence.

1 Plants will not grow unless _____

2 Houseplants do not grow outside because _____

3 Protect your outdoor plants if _____

4 Underline the verbs.

   The van raced down the high street, swerving from one side to the other.

5 Why were these verbs chosen? _____

Cross out the verbs. Write new verbs that make the animal sound angry.

6 The animal went down the street, looking around him.   _____ _____

7 The animal hopped from the branch and squeaked at the birds.   _____ _____

Add the capital letters and punctuation to the extract from a dialogue.

8   climb up here said the snake it is quite safe

9   what's that asked the farmer is it gold

10   oh thank you sobbed the girl

X There is only one correct answer.   X There is more than one correct answer.   **41**

Section 3   Test 11

A   WARM-UP

Underline the word that is **not** a real word.

1 careless tuneless tiredless homeless

2 readable bendable breakable dashable

3 prouder nearer painer driver

Continue the sentence so that it explains why.

4 She was excited _____

_____

5 He dashed out of the house _____

_____

6 The Moon is different from the Earth

_____

Add a short word to complete the longer word.

7 ___ t e n

8 a l ___ g

9 s o ___ t i m e s

10 b e c a ___ e

B   WORD WORK

1 Write the prefix beside its definition.

re pre anti

_____   again

_____   against

_____   before

Write two words starting with the prefix.

2 re   _____ _____

3 pre   _____ _____

4 anti   _____ _____

Write two different definitions.

5 gum   _____

_____

6 fit   _____

_____

7 pop   _____

_____

Complete the pairs of antonyms.

8 cheap and _____

9 boring and _____

10 awful and _____

C   SENTENCE WORK

Add a connective to link the two ideas.

1 "I did it _____ I thought you would be pleased."

2 "We can try _____ I'm not very hopeful."

3 "Let's tidy up _____ Mum is out."

Add the capital letters and punctuation.

4 buzzz what was that it was too loud to be a fly what could it be

5 they shouted no-one came they shouted again but still no-one came

6 it was a great big elephant an elephant in their front garden

Write the sentence again using at least three adjectives.

7 The woman carried a box with a lid.

_____

8 The castle was made of bricks and had five turrets.

_____

9 He wore a hat and a cloak made of feathers.

_____

10 How do the adjectives improve the sentences? _____

42   ☒ There is only one correct answer.   ☒ There is more than one correct answer.

A   WARM-UP

Finish the sentence.

1 Matt did not listen because _____

_____

2 Matt did not listen when _____

_____

3 Matt did not listen until _____

_____

Use the same word to complete both phrases.

4 wrist _____   _____ dog

5 traffic _____   toast and _____

6 _____ for sale   _____ as a pancake

7 The same letters are missing from all these
words. Write them in.

t ___ t l y   f r ___ t e n

m ___ t y   h ___ l ___ t

Add the missing syllables.

8 mis___ _____   bad luck

9 bell___ ____   shouting

10 thou_____   a large number

B   WORD WORK

Use the prefixes and suffixes to make four new
words from the word **fold**.

un re er able

1 _____   **3** _____

2 _____   **4** _____

Use two of the words you have made.

5 This box is _____.

6 I'll fold it and then _____ it.

Write a definition of the word in **bold**.

7 This box is **recyclable**.

_____

8 The door is **unhinged**.

_____

Underline the words that are wrongly spelt.
Write the correct spellings.

9 I tryed that onse but neva agayn.

_____ _____ _____ _____

10 The leefs swerl arownd the gardin.

_____ _____ _____ _____

C   SENTENCE WORK

Complete the sentence.

1 As _____, Mack began to smile.

2 If _____, it would be too late.

3 Before _____, the classroom door flew open.

4 When _____, he found Marie already waiting.

Rewrite the sentence so that it is clearer and more interesting.

5 The children went to see the thing. _____

6 The woman looked out at it all. _____

7 Explain how you made the sentences more interesting. _____

Proofread the text and write it correctly.

8 two mouses appeared squeak squeak they said _____

_____

9 help screamed Jo climbing on the chair _____

10 felix the cat creeped closer. _____

Now complete Section 3 of the Progress chart on page 46.

X There is only one correct answer.   X There is more than one correct answer.   43

Section 3 Writing task: Adventure story

Task
Write an exciting opening paragraph for an adventure story.

Hints

Before you start:

- Choose a title for your story – either **Mystery Towers** or **The Disappearing Box.**
- Write the title at the top of the box below.
- Think about an exciting event to start off your story.
- Decide how you will build up the excitement and sense of adventure.

As you write, think about:

- The words you choose.
- The sentences you write.

Title:

Check

- When you have finished, check through your writing.
- Have you remembered to use full stops and capital letters?
- Have you checked your spelling?

Section 3 Proofreading task: Letter to the head

Task

Proofread this letter from Class G to their headteacher.
Change anything that does not look or sound correct.

Hints

* Do the sentences sound right?
* Is the punctuation correct?
* Do all the spellings look right?

Deer mrs jenkins

We are riteing to tell you abowt our idea for raiseing muney to by the new playgrownd equipmunt we wuld like to hold a plant sale we will grow plants from seed and then sell them if we hold the plant sale afta scool we culd sell them to pupuls parents and teachas.

We think it is a reely good idea becuse we can grow the plants as part of our sciense project we has been lerning how plants grow we will ownly need a few packits of seads some pots and some compost.

We hopes you like our idea.

Class g

Extra

Write another very short letter to the head. Choose a different idea.

English Skills Book 2 Progress chart

Name	Class/Set
Teacher's name	Date

Instructions

Read the **'I can' targets** for the section you have just finished.
- Colour the circle **green** if you find it **easy** to do what is described.
- Colour the circle **orange** if you are **getting there**, but still need to work on it.
- Colour the circle **red** if you still find this a **difficult** thing to do.

If there are things that you still find difficult you can work on them in the next section or in the next book.

Writing sentences

'I can' targets	Section 1	Section 2	Section 3
I can write simple and compound sentences.	○	○	○
I can write sentences using words like **because**, **if**, **since** to link ideas.	○	○	○
I can write a series of linked sentences to develop an idea.		○	○
I can start sentences in different ways.			○

Using punctuation

'I can' targets	Section 1	Section 2	Section 3
I can use capital letters and full stops to start and end sentences.	○	○	○
I can use question marks and exclamation marks as necessary.	○	○	○
I can use commas in lists.	○	○	○
I can use capital letters for names and for effect.	○	○	○
I can use speech marks to show which words are spoken.		○	○
I can use commas between phrases in sentences.			○

Checking grammar

'I can' targets	Section 1	Section 2	Section 3
I can write in the past or the present tense.	○	○	○
I can check that the verbs in my sentences are correct (e.g., **was**, **were**).	○	○	○
I can write in the first or third person.			○

Understanding and choosing words

'I can' targets	Section 1	Section 2	Section 3
I can choose nouns carefully so as to be precise and give a clear picture.	○	○	○
I can choose interesting words rather than everyday words.	○	○	○
I can use a dictionary to check the spelling or meaning of a word.	○	○	○
I can use a thesaurus to find synonyms for common choices.	○	○	○
I can work out the meaning of a word from how it is used.	○	○	○
I can work out the meaning by looking at the parts of a word.		○	○
I can use adjectives to add interest.		○	○
I can choose words to fit different text types.			○
I can use a range of connectives to link events.			○

Spelling

'I can' targets	Section 1	Section 2	Section 3
I can segment words and choose the correct spelling of most phonemes.	○	○	○
I can spell compound words or words with more than one syllable.	○	○	○
I can spell tricky words (e.g. **school**, **people**, **thumb**, **half**).	○	○	○
I can spell words using prefixes (**un**, **dis**) and suffixes (**ful**, **ly**).	○	○	○
I can use the rules for adding **ing** and **ed** (e.g., **hopping**, **hurried**).	○	○	○
I can use rules to help me to spell plurals.	○	○	○
I can use apostrophes in shortened forms (e.g., **can't**).			○

Published by Schofield & Sims Ltd,
Dogley Mill, Fenay Bridge, Huddersfield HD8 0NQ, UK
Telephone 01484 607080

www.schofieldandsims.co.uk

Author: Carol Matchett
Carol Matchett has asserted her moral right under the Copyright, Designs and Patents Act, 1988, to be identified as the author of this work.

British Library Cataloguing in Publication Data
A catalogue record for this book is available from the British Library.

Commissioning and editorial project management by
Carolyn Richardson Publishing Services (www.publiserve.co.uk)

Design by **Ledgard Jepson Ltd**
Printed in the UK by **Wyndeham Gait Ltd**, Grimsby, Lincolnshire

English Skills 2 ISBN 978 07217 1176 8; Essential English Skills 2 ISBN 978 07217 1189 8

Schofield&Sims

the long-established educational publisher specialising in maths, literacy and science

English Skills provides graded questions that develop pupils' literacy skills at Key Stage 2. Key areas are constantly revisited, giving pupils the intensive practice that is essential if they are to become fully literate.

Every **English Skills** book is divided into three sections, each comprising 12 one-page tests. Some questions have more than one correct answer, and these are indicated using a simple key.

Every test page provides:
• Part A: 10 **Warm-up** questions – puzzles and other activities that focus on areas covered earlier
• Part B: 10 **Word work** questions – covering **spelling**, **word structure** and **vocabulary**
• Part C: 10 **Sentence work** questions – covering **sentence formation**, **punctuation** and **grammar**.

> **Pupils may answer the test questions independently or in pairs. Before they begin, check that they know how to handle the different question types.**

Each section also contains a **Writing task** and a **Proofreading task**, providing tailor-made contexts in which pupils may apply their developing skills. A **Glossary** defines literacy terms and a **Progress chart** helps them to monitor their own work.

English Skills **2**

English Skills 2 is for pupils who can use simple conjunctions to write compound sentences. They can spell correctly most high-frequency words and use spelling strategies to spell those that are less familiar. Designed for Year 3, this book may also be used with older or younger pupils.

It helps pupils learn to:
• use conjunctions (**while, when, because**)
• open sentences in different ways
• choose words for impact and precision
• use commas in lists and use " " and !
• add **ed** and **ing** correctly

• recognise **mis, non, re, pre, less, ness**
• adapt some spellings when adding a suffix
• apply the rules for plural spellings
• spell medium-frequency words
• use apostrophes in shortened forms.

The separate **English Skills 2 Answers** (ISBN 978 07217 1182 9) summarises the key **Focus** of each set of questions and gives answers to facilitate marking. The **Teacher's Guide** (ISBN 978 07217 1187 4) contains an **Entry test**, a **Group record sheet** and other valuable resources, helping you to use the series to its full potential.

The complete range of workbooks is as follows. A separate book of answers is available for each one.

English Skills 1 (for Key Stages 1 & 2)	978 07217 1175 1	**English Skills 4**	978 07217 1178 2
English Skills 2	978 07217 1176 8	**English Skills 5**	978 07217 1179 9
English Skills 3	978 07217 1177 5	**English Skills 6** (for Key Stages 2 & 3)	978 07217 1180 5

ISBN 978-07217-1176-8

MIX
Paper from responsible sources
FSC
www.fsc.org   FSC® C022534

ISBN 978 07217 1176 8
Key Stage 2
Age range 7–11 years
£2.95
(Retail price)

9 780721 711768

For further information and to place your order visit
www.schofieldandsims.co.uk or telephone 01484 607080